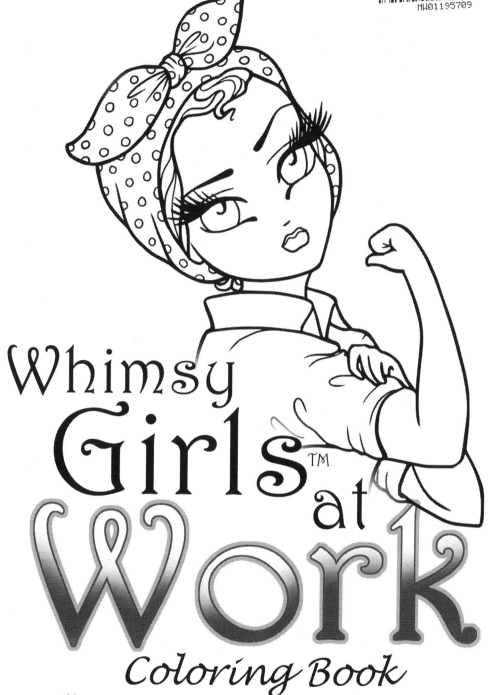

Whimsy Girls™ at Work

Coloring Book

Illustrated by Hannah Lynn

www.HannahLynn.com

Whimsy Girls at Work Coloring Book © HannahLynn.com

"Reef Study"

"On the Scene"

"Lunch Shift"

"Perfect Shot"

"Pearly Whites"

Made in the USA
Columbia, SC
04 May 2025

57520509R00070